Less Beaten Paths of America: Beyond Description – More of the Strange and Unique

David Kravetz

DEDICATION

This book is dedicated to the pioneers of the US roadways – those that built our highway systems and those that eventually built the support systems for the road-weary travelers. The expansive network of highways has made it possible for us to see and experience all parts of the country. And I also dedicate this to the visionary folks that built not only gas stations, but places to stop and eat, get a cold glass of ice water or cup of coffee, take a much needed restroom break and, while doing all of that, having a place for the kids to roam, stretch and play. The travel experience of the 21st Century can be attributed to those that created the roads and way stations along the way.

TABLE OF CONTENTS

ACKNOWLEDGMENTS

My gratitude can go out to hundreds, if not thousands of folks. Those close to me, such as my dear wife Julianne, who has put up with my quirky antics for over 40 years and to my children and grandchildren, who love my wanderlust and have a great time traveling with me. Then there are those close to me that have helped open doors for me in my travels – my sister Sherry and her husband Brian who always have a place for me to stay; my cousin Lewis who is always accommodating when I am in the Austin area; my dear friend and artist of my book covers Antsy McClain; travel author and mentor Tui Snider; Doug Kirby of Roadside America who has always been a cheerleader and constructive critic; my high school friends Jonathan Jensen and Russell Graves who have kindly opened their doors for me to stopover on my trips; Brad Sweeten of Kansas City; Michael Fisher of Georgetown, Texas; Ione Snyder and Carla Lockwood in California; Doug Wedding in Lexington, and many others. I strive to use all of my own photographs in my books, but sometimes I just need to get some from the outside. Special thanks to Lexington photographer Earl Hayes Raglin Sr. for the photograph on the back cover. My appreciation goes out to the **Cleveland Daily Banner** in Tennessee for permission to use a photo of artist Peter Toth taken by Daniel Guy. Caroline Porsiel of the **Atlanta Expat Magazine** was also kind enough to allow me to use one of her photos from a visit she made to Peter Toth's studio in Florida. Also, thanks to Marissa Noe for her photos. Finally, I want to give a shout out to all of the other travel bloggers and photographers out in the world that inspire me and keep my wanderlust alive when I am trapped in the confines of my hometown. This journey continues to drive me to new places and adventures. Thanks to you all!!

INTRODUCTION

In my previous book I covered my visits to many of the individual unique and quirky things I have seen across this country. Due to limitations in book size, many places were glossed over and many were not even covered. Such is the nature of a printed work.

In this third book, I am going to have a few more themes and will also visit a few places in depth. There are many places that are not just a one shot, one unique thing to see kind of place. Rather, they are more like destinations that have a number of great things to see and could take two or three hours of one's time in the visit. Many are multi-faceted in their offerings and provide a rich look at the artistic and creative endeavors of those that established the places. These will be covered in the first section of this book.

The second section of the book will feature bigger places...indeed, entire towns and places as large as towns that have a big theme. These are fun destinations and can take up one or two days of adventures if you give them the chance.

The final section will include some surprises.

It is my hope that you will enjoy the read and Enjoy the Ride!

SECTION I – DESTINATIONS

1 CARHENGE – Alliance, Nebraska

GLOWING SUN OVER CARHENGE

I touched upon *Carhenge* in my previous book as part of a section on car art. But there is so much more to this place than just a bunch of cars stacked up to replicate Stonehenge. In fact, there are a number of other car art displays, some unique sculptures made of car parts and even a complete collection of US License Plates hanging in the visitor's center.

Carhenge was the brainchild of Jim Reinders who had lived for a time in England and was inspired by the magnificence of Stonehenge. He wanted to replicate it in some way when he returned to the states and, in the summer of 1987 he was able to do it...with cars!

Reinders tried to match the exact measurements of Stonehenge in this work of art using thirty-nine cars placed in similar proportions to the monolithic structure in Wiltshire, England. Though one of a number of Stonehenge replicas, this is the only one made of cars. There are others made to be astronomically aligned and made of stone. Then there are the others, like Carhenge, that are made of items...including Strawhenge, Tankhenge, Fridgehenge and, as you will see in a later chapter in this book, there is even a "Thronehenge" made of old toilets.

CADILLAC HEELSTONE

The Carhenge portion of this sprawling ten acre site consists of 38 cars arranged in a circle measuring about 96 feet in diameter. Some of the cars are held upright in five foot deep pits, with the trunk end down. Arches were then formed by welding other cars on top of the supporting cars. Reinders even went so far as to add a heelstone, which is a 1962 Cadillac.

CARHENGE AS SEEN FROM THE VISITOR'S CENTER IN 2014

Though the main drawing card is the Carhenge sculpture, there are many additional sculptures that make up the Car Art Reserve. These include Reinders' "Ford Seasons," a sculpture comprised only of Fords and inspired by Vivaldi's Four Seasons.

Then there is the Spawning Salmon sculpture, made completely of car parts, that was created by Canadian artist Geoff Sandhurst. Other sculptures include a dinosaur and a flower, among a few others.

GEOFF SANDHURST'S "SPAWNING SALMON"

FORD SEASONS

Carhenge is located in Alliance, Nebraska and is one of Western Nebraska's major attractions. It is now owned by the city of Alliance, which promotes it heavily and provides the necessary upkeep to make it a fun and unique destination. Admission is free and the site is great to visit any time of the year.

2 PARADISE POINT – Scottsville, Kentucky

PARADISE POINT MARKETPLACE IN WINTER

During the break between Christmas 2017 and New Year's Day 2018 I took some of my family down to *Barren River Lake State Resort Park* in Lucas, KY. It was a wonderful time relaxing and going out around the lake and surrounding area looking at sunrises, sunsets and chasing down sandhill cranes, which had migrated in for the winter.

While there, we came across a fun little spot on US Highway 31E, heading towards Scottsville, Kentucky. During the winter, the place is closed, except on weekends. I first saw it on a Thursday and HAD to stop for a few photos as it was right down my quirky little alley.

THE HAPPINESS CAR

Called **Paradise Point Market Place**, it sits off the highway and on the edge of a funky little trailer park. Their building was surrounded by all sorts of quirky junk, old cars with signs, and more. I walked around gleefully to snap shots of all of the stuff. These folks really put the FUN in Funky! Meandering around the place we saw a car painted with happiness. There were little signs here and there, some junk and various other things. It was really something!

After walking around we noticed something else fun across the street. I think the photo below speaks for itself!!

We meandered across the street to check out the bus. After looking at the bus, which had all sorts of funny things going on, including a "Driving Comments" bumper sticker that had "No Thanks" painted over the original phone number. And there was a flamingo hanging out of the gas tank. Who needs a tiger in your tank when you can have a flamingo? I loved the humor.

After checking out the bus, I went back to the marketplace front door and saw that they would be open for breakfast on the weekends in the winter, so I decided we give them another visit on Saturday before we headed back home to Lexington.

Even around the front door there was enough eye candy to keep a quirky roadside blogger/photographer busy for quite a while. But my Sweetie (see photo below) wanted to get back to the hotel and get warm. It was quite cold out. So, we snapped a couple more pictures and were on our way back to the resort park.

Once Saturday morning came along, we checked out of the room and headed straight for Paradise Point. I just had to check out the inside of the place and possibly even try out their purported amazing homemade breakfast. WOW!

When I first got in, I introduced myself to the gal behind the counter and let her know I was a travel blogger and had to check it out. She introduced herself as Sebrina and then went on to tell me a bit about the place and made sure we knew about the GOOD food! She then went on to introduce me to her husband John...who looked EXACTLY how I assumed the proprietor of a place like this would appear!!

JOHN AND SEBRINA ERSKINE OF PARADISE POINT

I told John more about what I do since Sebrina was busy doling out her beautiful breakfast. I told him about my blog and my new book. John asked me to put my blog info on a postcard that had an Airstream trailer on it so he could visit later on. The Airstream post cadr led me to chuckle and mention that I was also the web guy for Antsy McClain and the Trailer Park Troubadours. To both my delight and amazement, not only had he heard of them, but he had a couple of CDs!!!

After the enlightening conversation, I walked around the shop and took a few photos before settling down to a wonderful breakfast burrito, homemade biscuits and gravy (Dr. John's Biscuits and Gravy) and a knock-em-dead cheesy hash brown casserole filled with potatoes, sour cream, cheese and topped with Sugar Frosted Flakes!!!

The shop favorite is always Dr. John's version of biscuits and gravy. He starts with *Steenbergen's* fresh pork sausage and well, the rest is his secret!   They make it all in advance and when it's gone, it's gone...

Needless to say, I was overwhelmed with breakfast and thrilled to meet John and Sebrina who epitomize happiness. And then there was the market place!!!

They carry the usual kinds of "gift shop" types of things in the shop -- you know, little towels with sayings, signs, coffee cups, trinkets. They also have a variety of offbeat and quirky...maybe even close to gag items. Walking around looking at the various and sundry items was enthralling...really, it was!

I really could have spent hours documenting and taking photographs, but some of the others in my party wanted to get on the road and head home. With tummies full and eyes bulging, we left. But I grabbed a few last shots...

Ultimately, we had a fantastic visit at Paradise Point. John and Sebrina are great hosts and some of the happiest folks you may never meet (unless of course you make your way to southern Kentucky to visit them!!) Be nice when you do or you may be ushered out....

3 BOWLIN'S "THE THING" – Dragoon, Arizona

ABOUT BOWLIN TRAVEL CENTERS

The Bowlin family of New Mexico has been running some sort of a travel center or exchange with the Southwestern Native Americans since 1912 when Claude M. Bowlin began trading with the New Mexico Native American groups.

In 1935 they built the *Old Crater Trading Post* near Bluewater, New Mexico. The road that led to this Trading Post later was paved and became part of the famed Route 66. Though it closed in 1973, they reopened along Interstate 40 nearby as *Bowlin's Bluewater Dairy Queen Travel Center*.

As the growth of the Interstate Highway System grew, so did the number of *Bowlin's Travel Centers*. By the 1980s, they had expanded their business into the outdoor advertising business (think billboards along the highway!). By the 1990s they had over 3000 billboards in five states.

After Claude passed away in 1974, his son Michael L. Bowlin took over the business. Today, with headquarters in Albuquerque, New Mexico, they operate a number of Travel Centers (actually 10 of them) in New Mexico and Arizona.

Seven of their Travel Centers are located along Interstate 10 in southern New Mexico and Arizona. Each of them have different themes, but most carry much of the same items... Native American artifacts, jewelry, a variety of souvenirs, fireworks, drinks, candy, snacks and fun stuff. The stores are clean and fun.

I have visited four of their 10 Travel Centers and, in my opinion, the best one is near Dragoon, Arizona... known as *THE THING?*

WHAT IS THE THING?

As you drive from El Paso, Texas to Tucson, Arizona on Interstate 10 you soon begin seeing billboards *advertising The Thing?*. I counted 15 signs before we even hit the Arizona border. Once into Arizona our eyes were barraged with the signs. In wide open spaces such as southern New Mexico, Wyoming, North and South Dakota, among others, these Trading Posts, Travel Centers, Tourist Traps (or whatever else you may call them) make sure you don't miss them. They are especially common near National Parks or other resort areas. (You will notice similar comments in my Wall Drug and Uranus sections below).

So, back to *The Thing?*. I believe it is the only Travel Center with a question mark in its name. This haven in the middle of the

Arizona desert not only has the amenities offered by other Bowlin's Travel Centers, but it also houses a museum, sells dinosaur and alien things and has a *Dairy Queen* attached (a common amenity to most of the Bowlin's nowadays.)

I have visited *The Thing?* three times in the past twenty years. Bowlin's has made sure to upgrade the facilities as well as the museum. The items for sale in the shop are both fun and interesting. The last time I visited, around 2007, there were no aliens or dinosaurs. But *The Thing?* was back there in the museum. *The Thing?* of 2019 is more fun, especially for the kids.

BEST RESTROOM SIGN IN THE COUNTRY

As for a description of *The Thing?*... sorry folks. I paid to see it and you should too. Why should I provide you a spoiler to the main reason for visiting and stretching? After you see The Thing in the museum, head on over to DQ for lunch and a treat. You'll forget you are in the desert for a few more minutes.

4 URANUS – Route 66, St. Robert, Missouri

Enter Missouri from the western border on Interstate 44 / Route 66 near Joplin, Missouri and you will begin seeing signs inviting you to *Pick Uranus, Visit Uranus, have Big Fun in Uranus, Explore Uranus*, etc.   I discovered Uranus in 2017 and cannot stop having fun with this place.

Its major draw is the **Uranus Fudge Factory**, which really does make fresh fudge (in fact, the employees are all called Fudge Packers). But, like many other "Tourist Traps,", they offer a variety of fun goods. Since this section of Route 66 is near the Ozarks, the theme here is not Southwestern Indian goods, but Hillbilly Goods and T-shirts celebrating the puntastic world of Uranus.

Those that know me well know that I am a major punster, and by-golly, Uranus provides a so many fun puns, it is a sure fire must-see destination if you are in this part of the country.

First of all, Uranus, Missouri is actually NOT a real incorporated town. It is located on State Highway Z in St. Robert, Missouri. It is the brainchild of Louie R. Keen, who brought the place to reality in 2015. Being a fun-loving sort, he created it with the puns in mind as a drawing card.

Besides the Fudge Factory, there is the Chicken Bones Bar & Grill, the Uranus Axehole (an Axe throwing facility), the Uranus

Sideshow Museum and, recently added, the Moonicorn Creamery & Funnel Cakery. The place has aliens, dinosaurs and even the wood cutout thingies for pictures...and your head goes in a special place for these!!! It is even home to the *Guinness Book of World Records* Title for the World's Largest Belt Buckle! Upon your visit, you will even be thanked by staff: *"Thank you for picking Uranus."*

5 WALL DRUG – Wall, South Dakota

Back in the 1970s I saw signs on the Highways and bumper stickers on cars with the question – *"Where the Hell is Wall Drug?"* I think that it has changed now to *"Where the Heck is Wall Drug?,"* but it's still the same thing.

I mentioned in an earlier section about Billboards advertising Travel Centers (or, well, Tourist Traps). I would venture to say that **Wall Drug** is the KING of this and has been for decades. There are Wall Drug signs noting how far away they are from the places in such distant locations as Morocco, Amsterdam and London. Legend has it that founder Ted Hustead hung a sign in the London Underground that proclaimed *Wall Drug* was only 5,160 miles away.

A WALL DRUG SIGN IN BLACK EARTH, MINNESOTA IN 2005

On another road trip, while driving across Minnesota and Wisconsin, I came across a Boot Shop in Black Earth, Minnesota with a Wall Drug distance sign hanging on it's wall.

Like the Bowlin's centers in New Mexico and Arizona, Dorothy and Ted Hustead got their start in the 1930s when they tried to establish Wall Drug as a successful drug store. The clincher for them was when Dorothy hand painted a sign and set it up on Route 16, the only nearby highway at that time. It simply said – *"Get a soda/get a beer/turn next corner/just as near/to Highway 16 and 14/free ice water/Wall Drug."* Even today they offer free ice water and five cent cups of coffee. Trust the billboards!

ONE OF DOZENS OF WALL DRUG BILLBOARDS ON I-90

Today Wall Drug has grown into a huge conglomeration of shops selling almost everything. There are many amenities for kids and even an 80 foot long huge dinosaur statue that can be seen from miles away on Interstate 90. There are many unique and quirky photo opportunities -- besides the huge dino, there is a jackalope that even holds adults, a buckin' bronc, a mini Mount Rushmore and an assortment of other fun things in the many shops and always.

MY SON SOLOMON ON THE JACKALOPE IN 2005

THE ICONIC WALL DRUG 80 FT. APATOSAURUS

Wall Drug made special efforts to get something better than a billboard when they hired South Dakota resident artist Emmet Sullivan (1887-1970) in the 1960s to erect the 80-foot-long concrete Apatosaurus that weighs more than 50 tons. It may not invite you for a 5 cent cup of coffee, but certainly a selfie with the big green dino should be enough of a lure.

ONE OF MANY IN-STORE SCENES AT WALL DRUG

6 APPLE VALLEY HILLBILLY GARDEN AND TOYLAND – Calvert City, Kentucky

KEITH HOLT WELCOMES VISITORS TO HIS HILLBILLY GARDEN AND TOYLAND

The *Apple Valley Hillbilly Garden and Toyland* was one of those *Roadside America* gems for me. I had to make a trip south and was looking for something interesting in southern Kentucky that I might hit along the way. I am always appreciative of the *Roadside America* team for their amazing gathering skills!

VISITING WITH KEITH HOLT IN THE HILLBILLY GARDENS IN 2017

Once I "discovered" this place, I called the owner, Keith Holt, to see if he would be around for me to visit. He was gracious and was absolutely excited about my visit. I was excited too. Though not sure what I was going to find, I was certain that I was going to have a fun adventure.

WELCOME TO HILLBILLY GARDEN

I had planned on about an hour for my visit, but it turned into a three hour tour by Keith, who has long hair, a nice old hillbilly hat and a lovely sense of humor. His pun-filled and fun-filled tour of the "*Hillbilly Garden*" was a real blast. Honestly, there are few places that can get much quirkier than this one. With the "Bumper Crop," "Thronehenge", shoe trees, Hillbilly "springs" and more, Keith has made what appears to be a junkyard into a PUNishing art display. Everything in the "Garden" has a story. And Keith tells all of the stories and only for donations.

Keith explained that he has had to fight with neighbors and Calvert City to keep his garden. Obviously, some people don't appreciate a place like his, but he draws in the media and many quirk-seeking tourists.

THRONEHENGE

THE BUMPER CROP

Once the garden tour was complete, it was on to Toyland. This is certainly not a museum. There is no rhyme or reason in the giant room filled with 1000s of toys. Like we did as children, Keith has mixed the different genres of toys to create stories. He has done this on a massive scale. There were toys in there that I had not seen in decades. Action figures galore. Cowboys and Star Wars figures were mingling with X-Men and cartoon characters. He still has 1000s more in a semi-trailer.

A VERY SMALL SECTION OF THE TOYLAND

EXTENSIVE STAR WARS COLLECTION

Finally, the small out-building right off of the highway used to be a café run by his grandfather. Lots of old history in there, including old soda and beer cans from all over, numerous travel books (including an original copy of one the Roadside America books, which is no longer in print.)

If you are in southwestern Kentucky on Interstate 24 (not too far southwest of Paducah) and anywhere near the junction to US 68, make plans to visit Keith and his Hillbilly Garden and Toyland. You will be glad you did!

7 STANDING ON THE CORNER – Winslow, Arizona

There are not many places that create a tourist attraction based on a song, but such is the case of Winslow, Arizona! Though it missed out on being included in the epic 1946 travel song *"Route 66,"* by Bobby Troup, it did get into the songs *"Take It Easy"* by The Eagles, and *"I've Been Everywhere"* by Johnny Cash.

Located on Route 66, the lyrics to *Route 66* include "Flagstaff, Arizona and don't forget Winona," but did not include Winslow. (Winona actually rhymed with Arizona, but there is not much of anything there and it is just about 40 miles west of Winslow. Both towns are on Route 66.

The saving grace for Winslow came in 1977 when Jackson Browne and Eagles front man Glenn Frey wrote the song "*Take It Easy*." It took nearly 22 years for Winslow to grab onto the notoriety that the song gave the old railroad town, which, at one time, was the largest town in Northern Arizona. Once Interstate 40 came rolling through Northern Arizona, Winslow was bypassed and the town was on the verge of shutting down.

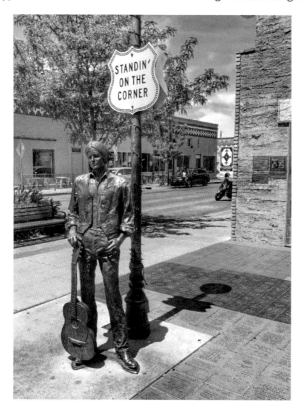

STATUE NICKNAMED "EASY" BY RON ADAMSON

However, with the song's lyrics, coupled with nostalgic interest in Route 66 (and that iconic song), Winslow decided to take a jump. Finally, on September 11, 1999 a corner in Winslow, right on Route 66 was dedicated as a tribute to the song. A small park was made that later included a statue representing Glenn Frey on the corner, a mural of a Flatbed Ford and a giant Route 66 logo that emblazons the main intersection.

THE WINSLOW CORNER MURAL COMMEMORATING THE SONG WAS PAINTED BY JOHN PUGH

The three other corners include shops that play Eagles music all day and have a variety of Route 66 and other memorabilia. It is estimated that over 100,000 visitors a year make their way to Winslow for the photo ops and souvenirs.

ONE OF THE SOUVENIR SHOPS IN WINSLOW

SOME PLACES TAKE ADVANTAGE, SUCH AS EARL'S 66 MOTEL

8 SHARKHEADS – Biloxi, Mississippi

In 1988 the *Discovery Channel* began their annual Shark Week television programming. Millions of viewers enjoy the amazing and oft-times scary shark-based programming. But, in Biloxi, Mississippi there is a place that celebrates sharks all year long and even features a giant shark head for an entrance in one of their TWO Biloxi shops.

The main shop, located on Biloxi Beach, was established in 1973 and is totally shark-themed with its 32 foot tall **Sharkheads** entry and a number of other large sharks. The other store – **Souvenir City** -- just down the street from the gigantic Sharkheads, features a giant gator head for its entrance.

SHARKHEADS 32 FOOT TALL SHARK HEAD

Another typical "tourist trap," this location features all-sorts of Biloxi Beach souvenirs, homemade fudge, etc. It claims to be the largest gift shop on the Mississippi Gulf Coast (and I would concur...it is massive!). Originally known as *T-shirt City*, they changed the name to **Sharkheads** in 2000 after installing the big shark head.

Sadly, like many Gulf Coast businesses, the shops were completely destroyed by hurricane Katrina in 2005. It took them until 2012 to rebuild and add a new 32 foot shark entrance. They were able to rebuild Souvenir City in 2009.

SOUVENIR CITY IN BILOXI, MISSISSIPPI

These places sell T-shirts, all kinds of fish things and shark things, custom airbrush t-shirts, hats, skim boards and more. And, of course, all of the fun foods that places like this all over the country have, especially their homemade fudge.

SHARKHEADS IN BILOXI

COLORFUL RESTROOMS AT SHARKHEADS

If you are on the Gulf Coast, you should definitely stop here for photo-ops and a unique shopping experience.

9 REAL GOODS – Hopland, California

In 2015 I made my way to northern California to attend the *Woodflock Festival* in Red Bluff. This is an annual Antsy McClain music and fun festival typically staged during the Memorial Day Weekend. I stayed with a friend in Santa Rosa before the event and we then drove the scenic route through Ukiah, Upper Lake, Nice and Williams. Along the way my friend highly recommended that we stop in Hopland for a unique shopping and viewing experience.

My first evidence that we were getting close was a big red sign on Highway 101 that said "Need to Pee?" After stopping to get a picture of the sign, we rolled into **Real Goods**, a kind of one-stop shop for those desiring to live off of the grid. In fact, the first retail solar panel ever sold in the United States was sold at Real Goods shortly after they were founded in 1978 by John Schaeffer.

A TRUE TOURIST DRAWING CARD?

I was privileged to meet John while there and was actually surprised to find that he was the author of the "*Solar Living Sourcebook.*" The book, originally published in 1982, was a great source of research for me in 1989 when I began working for *Asahi Solar Corporation*, Japan's largest supplier of Solar Water Heaters. We even made a solar oven with our children in Japan as a science project and baked a cake in it...with instructions from the book. While at *Real Goods* I picked up a new edition and had John sign it for me.

WITH SOLAR PIONEER / REAL GOODS FOUNDER JOHN SCHAEFFER

The shop is filled with all kinds of unique items for the homesteader – solar products, composting toilets, non-electric appliances and even a large glass covered beehive to see first hands how bees work. Of course, they sell beehive kits and tools. The shop itself was fascinating, but there was more.

Remember the "Need to Pee?" sign? Well, they have weird restrooms in the Eco Terra Center (used to be called the Solar Living Center). The walls of the bathrooms are made with recycled toilet tank lids and they even have a sign that explains the "Weird Restrooms."

Along with that there is a unique plumbing setup, a bicycle electricity generation station and a garden of vintage cars with trees growing through them (kind of mocking the famed drive-thru trees in the Sequoia National Forest).

And finally, take a walk along the pond to the giant metal sculpture called *"Horned Serpent"* by Diego Harris.

HORNED SERPENT AT REAL GOODS

10 YE OLDE CURIOSITY SHOP – Seattle, Washington

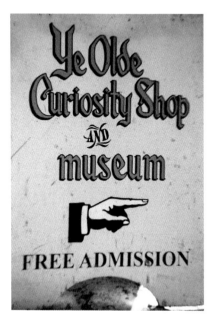

Seattle is a wonderful city to visit. There are beautiful mountains, the Puget Sound, the big market, boats, seafood and that famous Space Needle. But, tucked away along the pier walkway near downtown is another must see place called *Ye Olde Curiosity Shop*. This place is unlike any other touristy stop I have ever been to as it is loaded with the macabre and strange. Four legged chickens, two headed creatures and even replica shrunken heads.

This curious little shop was established in 1899 by a guy named Joseph Edward Standley. He served the timber workers, the mine workers and gold prospectors. Along with the goods he sold, Standley created a small museum of "1001 Curious Things" and many of them still remain. Natural oddities, taxidermy weirdness, mummies and other unique goodies.

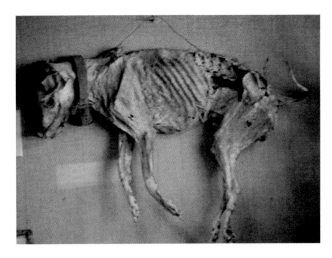

The shop is also home to a large amount of Northwest Native American art. The colorful woodworking and totem poles can be seen and purchased here.

CREEPY MERMAID HAS BEEN AROUND THE STORE FOR DECADES

My favorite object in the entire store is the Uber Creepy *Mermaid* or whatever it is called. This creepy guy has been hanging in the shop for nearly a century. The story of this creature goes back to the beginnings of the 20th Century when a fisherman named Smith shot and killed it off the shores of Duckabush, Washington.

There are few places where so many macabre items can be seen in one place. It is freaky. It is creepy. And it is fun. But they don't have fudge…..

If in Seattle, take a gander, if you dare….

11 QUICK LOOKS AT OTHER PLACES

-OLD TRAIL MUSEUM – Choteau, Montana

Venture your way to Glacier National Park in Montana and take a detour to the small town of Choteau on US Highway 89 to visit the *Old Trail Museum*. This is a great place to discover some of the natural and cultural history of the Mountain Front region. There are unique exhibits about grizzly bears, fossils and dinosaurs, including thee big dinosaur replicas perfect for photo ops.

There is a boardwalk you can take to art galleries, historical buildings and, finally, the Ice Cream Parlor. There is a small gift shop for the *Made in Montana* souvenirs, if you so desire. It really is a nice respite and admission is very reasonable at $2 per person...and well worth it! Located south of Browning and the entrance to Glacier National Park, it's a great place for the kids to get out and play for a few minutes before hitting the beautiful national park roadways.

-PP BY THE TEEPEE – Winslow, Arizona

Traveling on Interstate 40 eastbound (or, if you prefer, on US Route 66 where feasible), there are many fun trading post/gift shops and unique destinations, especially along the section from Flagstaff, Arizona to Gallup, New Mexico. In the heyday of Route 66, many Native American Trading Posts got their start. Some of these have faded away while others have either have moved to new locations along Interstate 40 or are still operating in their same locations.

TWIN ARROWS, ARIZONA

From Flagstaff, the first of these you might run across are the remains of the *Twin Arrows Trading Post*. All that remains now is a graffiti-covered shell of a building and the two famed giant yellow and red arrows in the ground. The arrows can be reached by taking exit 219.

Continue east on I-40 to Exit 239 and on the south side of the Interstate you will see the remains of what used to be the *Meteor City Trading Post*. This place has gone through two transformations and is currently in a big state of disrepair. However, it appears that there is another group trying to bring it back to life. The iconic domed building surrounded by a couple of Teepees made for an interesting stop back in the day.

One of my more interesting favorites along this route is the *Navajo & Hopi Indian Arts & Crafts shop* east of Winslow on Exit 257. I had to stop here for some photos because the big billboards outside of Winslow advertised **PP by the TP** and I had to see what it was all about. And, sure enough, there is a Porta-potty sitting right next to a Teepee. I didn't venture into the gift shop on my June 2019 visit since I had many other stops and had to get to Albuquerque that evening. But, it was worth the photo stop.

Further along the way are many other Native American Trading Posts, each with its own selling point. These include the famed *Jack Rabbit Trading Post* at Exit 269, the *Geronimo Trading Post* east of Joseph City, the *Painted Desert Indian Center* east of Holbrook, the *Chief Yellowhorse Trading Post* in Lupton and *Chee's Indian Store* near Sanders and finally the now closed but oh so interesting *Fort Courage Trading Post* in Houck.

WIGWAM MOTEL IN HOLBROOK, ARIZONA

And don't hesitate to take a swing through Holbrook to see dozens of dinosaurs and the iconic Wigwam Village Motel, a throwback to the 1950s and still in operation. There are only three of these still remaining in the U.S. – *The Wigwam Village #2* in Cave City, Kentucky; *The Wigwam Village Motel #6* in Holbrook, Arizona and *The Wigwam Village Motel #7* in Rialto, California (also on Route 66).

-RA66IT RANCH – Route 66 in Staunton, Illinois

RA66IT RANCH IN STAUNTON, ILLINOIS

WITH OWNER RICH HENRY AND ONE OF HIS RABBITS

AN OLD SIGN FROM THE JACK RABBIT TRADING POST IN JOSEPH CITY, AZ

Henry's Ra66it Ranch (the 66 replaces bb…intentional) celebrates Route 66 and the people along the highway with its emporium of highway and trucking memorabilia that includes a collection of Campbell's "Humpin' to Please" trailers next to a replica of a vintage gas station. It is also a celebration of rabbits.

Henry started his own little corner of Route 66 in Illinois back in 1994 opening it up as *Henry's Route 66 Emporium*. But, in 1999 his daughter had some problems with her pet rabbits and that is when Henry changed things to the *Ra66it Ranch*. From actual living rabbits hanging around in the shop to his celebration of Amarillo's *Cadillac Ranch* and its buried cars with his 7 half-buried VW Rabbits and then a giant sit-on fiberglass rabbit in the front, this is a place for Route 66 style rabbit fun. Make sure that you visit *The Tale of Ears*, a rabbit graveyard with over 30 tiny tombstones remembering some of the earlier rabbit residents of Ra66it Ranch.

HENRY'S VERSION OF A SIT-ON RABBIT

Of course, Henry has a selection of souviners...both rabbit-related and Route 66 related. And, while there, grab a bottle of Route Beer 66 to cool off.

-CHEESE SHOPS – US 51 in Central Wisconsin

Route 66 may be the place for Native American Trading posts and other memorabilia, but US Highway 51 (and nearby Interstate 90) from Beloit, Wisconsin all the way north to Minocqua could most definitely be called the *"Cheese Highway"* because of all of the cheese shops. And, to add fun to a trip like this are all of the big fiberglass statues along the way including a giant bulldog, giant mice, giant cows and even a famous Pink Elephant. (I covered all of these in my previous book.

GIANT MOUSE OUTSIDE OF THE CORNELLIER SUPERSTORE IN BELOIT

Like the many other touristy gift shops along US highways, these cheese shops sell cheese, cheese products, sausages and, my favorite, the squeaky and flavorful cheese curds. But, they also sell all sorts of cheesy souvenirs, including the now well-known Cheese Head Hats, key chains, stickers, magnets, etc.

MURAL DEPICITING CHEESE MAKING OUTSIDE OF EHLENBACH'S CHEESE
CHALET IN DEFOREST, WISCONSIN

CHEESEHEADED RACOON IN WISCONSIN

And, for interest sake, when you get to Wausau, Wisconsin, take a detour on Wisconsin 73 and head over to Colby, Wisconsin to get a photo of the Historical Marker about Colby Cheese.

-PAPA JOE'S STOP & GO – Crescent Junction, Utah

Out in the middle of nowhere in Utah is the small highway intersection called Crescent Junction at the junction of I-70 and

US 191. There is really not much there and it is basically a tourist-trappy stopover point for folks heading to and from the lovely canyons of Moab. At the center of it all is Papa Joe's Stop & Go. Called a C-Store (short for Convenience Store), Papa Joe has a number of unique "attractions" in store. He also has gas pumps, but that is probably one reason NOT to stop. But, for the other things, it is a fun stopover.

He has a replica of the *Mystery Machine* from Scooby-Doo and an assortment of alien cut-outs along with all of the kitschy knick-knacks that one might want.

When I visited in 2018, Joe was just opening up a second shop in the neighboring building and was calling it *"Bad Ass Joe's"* which is going to be Beef Jerky shop with selections from all over the country. He plans on giving it a UFO/Alien Theme.

BAD ASS JOE'S BEEF JERKY

LIKE SKELETON STUFF - JOE HAS IT!

JOE ALSO HAS SOME GNASTY GNOMES

Obviously, the place has restrooms, lots of snacks and drinks, quite a few wacky souvenirs and they also sell *Crop Circle Popcorn* in a variety of fun flavors, not to mention all of that Beef Jerky.

-LOST RIVER TRADING POST – Wardensville, West Virginia

A new entry in the world of touristy shops is the **Lost River Trading Post** in the small town of Wardensville, West Virginia. Though smaller than most shops that cater to traveling tourists, Lost River is a unique shop with a horde of West Virginia goodies, some unique menu items for breakfast, handmade home décor items and even a big orange cow with a cowboy hat and guns that they call Cowlamity Jane. They also have a small selection of unique food items from local manufacturers, a large selection of custom beers and ales from all over the US (no, I don't partake, but there are many unique ones), and more. I was really impressed with the many offerings of regionally handmade crafts, candles, jewelry, dishware and toys.

COWLAMITY JANE

The shop may look small from the outside, but there are lots of things in there.

HANDMADE GOODS AND ANTIQUES GALORE

A HUGE SELECTION OF BEERS AND ALES FROM ALL OVER THE COUNTRY

EVEN HAVE A FEW WILD ANIMALS TO WELCOME THE UNWARY VISITOR

All of their small selection of food offerings are made when ordered. Below is their semi-vegetarian breakfast frittata with a homemade biscuit, eggs and vegan sausage (which was actually amazingly yummy!)

-JUNGLE JIM'S INTERNATIONAL MARKET – Cincinnati, Ohio

One final must-see destination is the massive **Jungle Jim's International Market** located in the Fairfield area of Cincinnati. Founded in 1971 by "Jungle" Jim Bonaminio, the store grew from a small fruit stand into a behemoth 300,000 square foot (that's 6.5 acres!!!) of floorspace with nearly 200,000 items.

EXOTIC MEATS FROM AROUND THE WORLD

This is truly a shopping experience like none other as the store is also like a theme park inside with numerous animatronic statues and many unique and unusual displays around the store. All sorts of international goods are sold there. For instance, do you like butter? They have dozens of varieties from all over the world. There is even an "Adult Oriented Hot Sauce" collection.

Perhaps the most unique attraction is the restrooms in the back of the store. The entrances are designed as portapotty entrances, but lead into large, clean restrooms. With photo ops on nearly every aisle and with a huge souvenir area, this store will rival any in the country for uniqueness and character. It's not grocery shopping, it's an adventure well worth the visit.

WORLD FAMOUS RESTROOMS AT JUNGLE JIM'S

DOZENS OF LARGE ANIMALS AT JUNGLE JIM'S

A SAMPLE OF THE INSIDE OF JUNGLE JIM'S

SECTION II – BIGGER PLACES

THE BIGGER PICTURE

Sometimes a gift shop and unique shopping experience are not enough. Some places have literally "gone to town" to make the entire town a theme location. Perhaps Las Vegas is the best example of that, but will not be included in this book. However, there are other smaller and fun examples of how towns have added a unique theme to bring in the visitors. Following are a few of the places I have been to.

12 GO TO HELL – Hell, Michigan

Many people have heard the term "Cold as Hell." Visit **Hell, Michigan** in the winter, and you'll get it…. Fortunately, I visited Hell in the summer. Hell is one of those places that you really have to intend to go to because it is not really a place to pass through on your way to somewhere else.

Hell is a small community about three miles southwest of Pinckney, Michigan via Patterson Lake Road. Supposedly named by town founder George Reeves in 1841 when someone asked him what he thought they should name the place. His response was something along the lines of "I don't care. You can name it Hell for all I care."

In the age of tourism, the folks in Hell have done all they can to draw tourists. From the website gotohellmi.com to the miscellaneous Hell-themed shops and eateries, it is certainly a fun place to drive out of your way to.

If you go to Hell, make sure to get a post card and send it from the Hell Post Office. It is not an official Post Office anymore, but they do stamp it from Hell. If you know what day you will be there, you can also apply to be the official Mayor of Hell for a day, you can get married on Hell Creek and you can even buy a square inch of Hell and thus own a piece of Hell. Finally, get your *Been to Hell* bumper sticker or an assortment of other Hell merchandise.

My advice to you? Go to Hell!!

13 HO HO HO – Santa Claus, Indiana

Don't like Hell? How about something more Christmasy? A drive through southern Indiana on Interstate 64 will take you by the exit for *Santa Claus, Indiana*. Yes, you can celebrate Christmas year around in this fun little town.

Obviously, there are Christmas ornaments and other Christmas goodies, but there are also plenty of fun places for pictures including the Santa Claus Post Office, a giant Santa on a hill, and a variety of other Santas, snow men, etc. And, if you get the right day, you can visit the real Santa Claus and chat with him whether you are naughty or nice.

The town has Santa Claus everything. There is a Santa Claus Fire Department and yes, there is a Santa Claus police (especially for the naughty!). Don't commit a crime in this town or you may end up in the Santa Claus jail too!

Santa Claus has a giant candy store and the old Santa Claus post office which has fun kids activities.

GRANDKIDS ALL MADE THE GOOD LIST (PHOTO BY MARISSA NOE)

GOOD BOY SUMOFLAM

DOESN'T HAVE TO BE CHRISTMAS TO VISIT SANTA IN SANTA CLAUS, IN

Look carefully in town and you can find the Grinch too....

CHRISTMAS STORY HOUSE – CLEVELAND, OHIO

While on the subject of Christmas, I will add a short note that you can go to Cleveland to visit the house that was featured in the movie *"A Christmas Story"* and also get Christmas ornaments including the famed Leg Lamp and a Red Rider BB Gun. There is admission to go in the house, but you can certainly park in front of it and get a shot of the house. And that famed Leg Lamp is still in the window!

14 TROLLTOWN USA – Mt. Horeb, Wisconsin

There may not be a "Troll Bridge" in Mount Horeb, Wisconsin, but there is the *"Trollway."* Everything in the town of just over 7000 is about Trolls. The place certainly has small-town charm and a delightful array of small shops and eateries scattered throughout the whimsical community.

Going back to the 1850s, Mount Horeb has celebrated its Norwegian heritage. As a continuation of this heritage, in the 1980s the town transformed itself into the *Troll Capital of the World*. Main Street Mount Horeb is now referred to as the Trollway and a drive through town will grant visitors the opportunity to see close to 40 hand-carved trolls throughout the town. These humorous larger-than-life statues (some are 12 to 16 feet tall) are each unique and fun.

After visiting and mingling with all of the town trolls, make sure to stop into the *Grumpy Troll Brew Pub* for some tasty grub, more photo ops and, if you are a beer enthusiast, you can get samples of their many brews.

15 ALIENS EVERYWHERE – Roswell, New Mexico

Talk about a town that really brings in an out-of-this-world element to create a theme for the community!! Roswell has little aliens, big aliens, space ships, alien-themed soda machines and even a space-ship shaped McDonald's.

Roswell was not always a home to UFOs and aliens. It got its start in 1869 when two adobe buildings were built to become the community's general store, post office and small hotel. Business Van C. Smith had moved from Omaha, Nebraska to start this settlement and, in August 1873, he became the town's first postmaster. His father was Roswell Smith, a lawyer in Lafayette, Indiana and that is where the name comes from.

Jump to 1947 and Roswell's place in history was made when there was an alleged UFO crash that included a spaceship and its alien occupants. Since that time, and especially beginning in the 1970s, the town has taken full advantage of this alleged, and to this day, controversial event. The entire town is decked out with museums, tourist shops and all sorts of alien-themed eateries and wall art, all with the intent of bringing in the tourists interested in UFOs, paranormal activities, science fiction and aliens.

The Truth may be out there somewhere, but I am not sure if it is really in Roswell. But, you can certainly get your "alien" on there.

VISIT EARTH – EARTH, TEXAS

If you have gone as far as Roswell for an out-of-this-world adventure, you might as well go an addition 150 miles to make your way back to Earth... Earth, Texas that is. It is basically a straight run northeast on US Highway 70 through Portales, New Mexico and Muleshoe, Texas.

Earth, Texas was established in 1924 after William E. Halsell laid out the townsite. Originally, Halsell wanted to name the town Fairlawn, but it was determined that Texas already had a town by that name. The name Earth was apparently submitted by Ora Hume Reeves who became the owner of the town hotel.

16 CELEBRATING STAR TREK – Vulcan, Alberta

Keeping with the spacey subject matter, how about a trip up north to Canada to the town of Vulcan, Alberta? This town celebrates its unique name by having a Star Trek theme throughout the small community.

Vulcan is located midway between Calgary and Lethbridge in the prairies of southern Alberta. It was named by a surveyor for the Canadian Pacific Railroad in 1915 after the Roman God of Fire – Vulcan. But, as citizens of Vulcan, they found it perfectly logical to create a place that would draw 1000s of Star Trek fans from all around the world thus making it possible for them to hopefully live long and prosper.

THE VULCAN TOURISM AND TREK STATION

The main attraction in town is the *Vulcan Tourism and Trek Station* which is designed to look like a space station. Go inside for various dioramas about Star Trek. There is even a photo op where you can change in Star Trek clothes and take photos with standups of old Star Trek stars.

Also, throughout the town there are various other unique Star Trek items including a Bust of Spock that is on display, a mural that includes all of the doctors from the various Star Trek programs and, of course, a large statue of the original Starship Enterprise. There is the *Enterprise Café* and all of the town parks and venues that have signs with the Star Trek logo. Even the town of Vulcan uses a Star Trek logo! The Vulcan Public Library has a Starship in its logo, there are signs in Vulcan, Klingon and English. Even the stores carry unusual Star Trek themed items. Since I last visited in 2007, the town has also installed a two-person transporter. If that is not enough, every July the town has a huge convention called Vul-Con that quite often has stars from Star Trek visiting. Visit, live long and prosper!

WITH MY FRIEND CRAFTY JACK AT THE STARSHIP STATUE IN VULCAN

17 SCREAMING HEADS AND MIDLOTHIAN CASTLE – BURK'S FALLS, ONTARIO

MIDLOTHIAN CASTLE NEAR BURK'S FALLS, ONTARIO

Admittedly, *The Screaming Heads* and *Midlothian Castle* is not a small town, but I include it in this section chiefly due to the size of the place, which is as big as a small town.

Like Carhenge, The Screaming Heads is a giant art installation. But, unlike Carhenge, you definitely need a car to get around. The main attractions, the Screaming Heads of Midlothian Ridge, are over 100 twenty foot tall concrete monuments created by artist and retired teacher Peter Camani. They are spread out over nearly 310 acres of fields, woods and ponds. And they are truly a creepy, amazing sight. It is also the home of the eerie Midlothian Castle, which even has its own dungeon.

The Screaming Heads, some as tall as 20 feet and weighing 30 tons, are scattered throughout the property in what appears to be random placement. Some are round, spooky looking heads that appear to be screaming. Others are more like ghosts with a pointed head. Really quite interesting.

Then there is the Midlothian Castle, which is adorned with a scary two-headed dragon at the top and a gate with a giant spider-web and spider on it. Around the fence are the See/Say/Hear No Evil heads to greet visitors.

Getting here is half the fun as Burk's Falls is located about 165 miles north of Toronto and about 37 miles west of the amazing Algonquin Provincial Park. It can be accessed from Ontario Highway 11. Once in Burk's Falls, you need to head southwest on Ontario 520 to Midlothian Road and continue a few miles. I promise that you won't miss the place.

HINT: You might want to avoid mid-September unless you are a festival-going type. The massive Harvest Festival is held there annually and brings in 1000s of people to celebrate the harvest in the midst of all of the Screaming Heads.

SECTION III – THE TRAIL OF THE WHISPERING GIANTS

18 THE WHISPERING GIANTS

PETER WOLF TOTH MAKING A REPAIR TO HIS CHEROKEE CHIEFTAN IN CLEVELAND, TN 2018. (*PHOTO BY DANIEL GUY & USED WITH EXPRESS PERMISSION FROM THE CLEVELAND DAILY BANNER, CLEVELAND, TN***)**

The Trail of the Whispering Giants is a cross country collection of huge wooden sculptures created by Hungarian-born American artist Peter Wolf Toth. Each is a tribute to the indigenous peoples of North America. His goal was to carve at least one in every state in the United States.

As I was working on this book in August 2019, I had the wonderful opportunity to speak with artist Peter about his monumental statues honoring Native American chiefs and leaders.

He explained that he was born in Hungary, but came to the United States at a young age, landing in Akron with his family. As he grew older he grew interested in Native American culture and sought for ways to honor them. He became a self-taught sculptor, using a hammer and chisel to work with stone. He told me that his first sculpture was in stone in La Jolla, California. He wanted to do another in stone near his home in Akron but, as he explained to me,

"It was in a remote location and really not visible to many. I wanted to make these to honor the Native Americans, so I felt that making them from local trees in all of the states would honor them best."

CHIEF WACINTON - PADUCAH, KENTUCKY

Unlike many wood artists, Toth does not use a chainsaw. Though he does use some electric tools for sanding and otherwise, his chief tools remain the hammer and the chisel.

Peter also want to make it very clear that he has donated his time and the statues in each state as another way to honor these original native Americans and their history and heritage.

Since that rock sculpture in 1972, Toth has created 74 different sculptures, including one in each state of the United States and some in Canada. He has also done one in his birth country of Hungary. Some of these have disappeared due to storms, age, rot or otherwise. When possible, Toth has strived to reproduce those that have disappeared or become damaged. The photo above is of him working on weather damaged sculpture in Tennessee.

By 1988, Peter had finally carved out at least one statue in each of the 50 United States, with his 50th being in Hawaii. Since then he has continued to create and/or repair others. His most recent completion was #74 in 2009 in Vincennes, Indiana.

SUMOFLAM WITH IKALA NAWAN IN ASTORIA, OREGON

In my travels I have made my way to 13 of these amazing sculptures so far, many of which are about 20 to 30 feet tall. The most recent one I saw was in Winslow, Arizona in June 2019. This is one of his tallest and stands more than 40 feet tall. A man named David Schumaker made it his mission to get to as many of these as possible and has actually created a website dedicated to his findings. He features photos and details of 57 different sculptures.

PETER TOTH AT HIS FLORIDA STUDIO IN APRIL 2018. (*PHOTO BY CAROLINE PORSIEL AND USED WITH EXPRESS PERMISSION BY THE PHOTOGRAPHER AND THE ATLANTA EXPAT MAGAZINE*)

On the following pages are photos of those that I have visited along with their name, location, and the official identification number as noted in Wikipedia and on David Schumaker's website.

L - #61 - HO-MA-SJAH-NAH-ZHEE-GA IN OTTAWA, IL - CREATED IN 1989
R - #68 IN IOWA FALLS, IA - CREATED IN 1999 (REPLACED #28)

L - #21 - NANTICOKE - CREATED IN 1976 IN OCEAN CITY, MD
R- #37 IN IDAHO FALLS, ID - CREATED IN 1980

L- #32 IN RED LODGE, MT – CREATED IN 1979
R - #69 - CHIEF LITTLE OWL IN BETHANY BEACH, DE - CREATED IN 2002
(REPLACED #22)

#52 - CHIEF WASATCH - MURRAY, UT

L - #54 - DINEH - LAS CRUCES, NM - CREATED IN 1986
R - #33 - WINSLOW, AZ - CREATED IN 1980

1 L - #57 - IKALA NAWAN - ASTORIA, OR - CREATED IN 1987
R - #16 - HOPEWELL GIANT - CREATED IN 1975

L - #17 - CROOKED FEATHER - OCEAN SPRINGS, MS - CREATED IN 1975
R - #62 - CHIEF WALKS WITH THE WIND - UTICA, IL - CREATED IN 1989

HANGING WITH THE UTICA, IL GIANT IN 2018

19 ENJOYING THE RIDE EVERYWHERE

And this completes Book 3 of a planned 12 books on my back roads travels across America. The next in the series will be titled "**Mural Towns, Graffiti Walls and Wall Art**" and will feature full color photos of some of the hundreds of amazing murals I have discovered throughout the United States and Canada.

Less Beaten Paths of America Series:

Book 1: Unique Town Names (published 2017)
Book 2: Quirky and Offbeat Roadside Attractions
Book 3: Beyond Description – More of the Strange and Unique
Book 4: Mural Towns, Graffiti Walls and Wall Art
Book 5: Scrap Metal Giants and Other Road Art
Book 6: Unique Museums and Other Unique Places
Book 7: Fun, Tasty and Offbeat Eateries and Diners
Book 8: US National Parks and Monuments
Book 9: Geologic Wonders
Book 10: The Highways of America
Book 11: Buildings, Bridges and Other Structures
Book 12: Other Fun Stories From The Road

ABOUT THE AUTHOR

David Kravetz, 63, resides in Lexington, KY and is the owner and creative mind behind Sumoflam Productions, where he works with dotcoms, writes blogs and does nature photography. He currently manages the movie and TV databases for ComicBook.com and PopCulture.com, both of which are part of the CBS Interactive family.

In his spare time, he is a freelance travelographer and photojournalist and focuses on the normal, the wacky, the wonderful and the quirky things of this wide world.

His most popular blog is his *Less Beaten Paths* blog which has over 350 posts about offbeat locations and back roads travel. He also writes a couple of other blogs which cover a variety of topics.

Mr. Kravetz has photo sites that feature many of his best nature photography photos. You can also see thousands of his trip photos on his Sumoflam SmugMug site. His photos have been used in advertising, newspapers and even on a couple of magazine covers.

Sumoflam, as he is known to thousands of friends around the US and other parts of the world, has a passion for traveling and has been to all 50 of the states in the United States, as well as five provinces in Canada, numerous states in Mexico, the Philippines, China and South Korea. He lived in Japan for 6 years and is fluent in Japanese.

He is the father of five and has TEN grandchildren who call him Grampz. He has been married to his lovely wife Julianne for more than 40 years. He will admit that he truly Married Up!!

Made in United States
Orlando, FL
05 April 2022